GW00691727

LYRICALLY JUSTIFIED

By Urban Word Collective
Volume 1

Lyrically Justified
By Urban Word Collective

© 2016 Urban Word Collective
Individual copyright is retained by the writers at the time of publishing
Compiled by Shaun Clarke on behalf of Urban Word Collective
Cover design by Shamile Haline and Arkbound

ISBN: 9780993526558

First published in 2016 by Arkbound Ltd (Publishers)

* * *

*Arkbound is a social enterprise that aims to promote social inclusion,
community development, sustainability and artistic talent. It sponsors
publications by disadvantaged authors and covers issues that engage
wider social concerns.*

*Arkbound fully embraces sustainability and environmental protection. It
endeavours to use material that is renewable, recyclable or sourced
from sustainable forest.*

Arkbound
Backfields House
Upper York Street
Bristol BS2 8QJ
England

www.arkbound.com

Dedicated to the masses, and to our loved ones. While we remember where we came from, in an uncertain world, may we grow and create to one day soon find a place worth being in…

ACKNOWLEGEMENTS

Thanks to anyone who supports this book in any way. To Harry Lotta and Saiqa Rehman for allowing to use this fitting title. To our mothers and fathers, brothers and sisters, blood related or otherwise who lend a hand in their own way. Thanks to Khadijah Ibrahim, (one busy sister), for her time and effort. To Nadinne Dyen, and Freedom Project, and to Arkbound Publishers.

PREFACE

This is life from the perspective of a range of artists - a collective of writers from poetic and musical backgrounds, with something to say about the state of things. The idea is that anyone can pick this up and learn something, or at least be encouraged to raise questions about what we think we are doing and how things might be improved.

A symbol of unification in the face of common problems, Lyrically Justified is full of reality, commentary, and humour. It is a forum of UK based artists who on this shared platform have a space to express themselves beyond their usual art form.

While remaining independent in their contribution, these writers of our time have joined forces as a team of community heroes. They're about word power and righteousness, addressing confusion, offering alternative perspectives. They are a sub-stream, with roots in a variety of urban cultural and artistic forms.

Such a book is not necessarily for the faint hearted. Although offensive language is omitted, content is raw and rebellious. Do not only expect traditional genre. The chosen ones are conscious ones; the new age is timeless. We know the world is imperfect and are motivated to do something about it, to speak out. We share the goal of educating our own, addressing imbalance and redressing inequalities. Ultimately we want a better world. We're only partial to who we are, where we're from, and the values we represent. We are open to be challenged and have faced up to the terrible, knowing it's not too late to influence destiny, through words, since more than chance brought us together.

Contributing artists - in no particular order (See back pages for brief biographies)

1. Testament
2. Nadinne Dyen
3. Michael Jenkins aka Lowdose
4. Shaun Clarke aka Shaun MC
5. Denetta D3 Copeland
6. Redeyefeenix
7. Saiqa Rehman aka Lightning Sykes
8. J. Bravo
9. Steve Duncan
10. Axsom Nelson aka Matry Mcfly
11. Empress Imani
12. Idren Natural aka InI oneness
13. Edson Burton
14. Louis Mcintosh
15. Saju Ahmed
16. David Okwesia aka Full Flava
17. Silver Finger Singh
18. Justin Swaby aka Wordgineer
19. Princess Emmanuelle aka EmpresS*1
20. Karabo Moruakgomo aka Kayb
21. Shamile Haline

Foreword by Khadijah Ibrahiim

Generating this type of collection gives a platform to writers, who are without a doubt talented live artists and performers. From the stage to the page - built on passion - this collection shows us a willingness coming out of each person to share what they have. Their words speak of society, of personal experience, struggle, freedom and rights. It's current and necessary for the time we are living in.

This is a new generation of poets, singers and word smiths speaking for themselves. The collection rings out verses that shine in the hearts and mind of each writer who are shaping and reshaping time and place.

Khadijah Ibrahiim was born in Leeds, England. She's is the Artistic Director of Leeds Young Authors and the Producer of Leeds Youth Poetry Slam festival. Another Crossing (Peepal Tree Press), is her latest poetry collection.

Contents

PROLOGUE

By Shaun Clarke

Shout out! To them who aim to fight for what's right, and keeping it tight with love kept in sight.

Life as it is, as it was, and how it will be. Shouting all rappers, rhymers, tellers of truth and justice, as much as they know. Those who hear the calling, see the rainbows and feel the push, and those who react to suppressive nonsense.

All raconteurs and connoisseurs, here we are at last, communicating and remonstrating, for a cause - pro-acting to save ourselves, our souls, our children, our world. We heard the alarm and now assemble, motivators motivated by love, reactivated by provocation, challenging pontification, rarely reacting and mostly responding.

We're an Iration-inter-nation, fed on sorts of Ital vegetation sensations, filled to brims with inspiration. The spirit of the whole is found within, where we are immense power.

Reaching out to take a hand so we can hold strong, a force of one, putting it out there to be considered, offering experience that could change lives and the world for the better. Sometimes it's one for all...

Those who recognise, if need be, we must be there for each other. Survival is our master and nature our mistress. To the taunted who aim for construction over mindless disruption, and self-destruction. Duly, we move sideways, backwards and even duck when necessary in order to move forward, superseding old expectation, stereotypes and the like...

Here we stand ready and willing to embrace a new day.

LYRICALLY JUSTIFIED

By Saiqa Rehman,
aka Lightning Sykes

(Roots of the open-mic night, which inspired the name of this book)

Year 2004, we opened the door
Started a revolution where music is the cause,
Having no boundaries, no pigeon holes
Bring together all genres,
Becoming a musical force.
We united, yes we stand up and fight as one,
Dropping bombs of dreams, Harry's the lion's sun
Give us what you got, we're not fazed by fun
If you got what it takes, we give you a run,
As score the pen to page,
Go to enlist all those who have played
It scorches to flames,
From the greats, to those who felt astray
they took the stage, felt afraid
Entertained and engaged,
Open minds blew us away.

We've been blessed
Thank you for this chance today
Building up self-esteem,
Self-belief is a vital key
to see and unlock your dream,
Keeping it alight as we live 'n breathe,
Visions and thought lead me to my dreams

With hope and faith, now its reality.

Yes, I'm lyrically justified
When I took the oath to love and live my life,
And always reach for the light, I'm lyrically justified,
As I stand and do it with pride
Burning with the desire for life
Yes, I'm lyrically justified when I take the **mic**
Walking the path that leads me to new heights.
I'm lyrically justified when I redefine my justice in life
With no fear in sight,

We're lyrically justified when we stand up and say what's
right,
Using verbal vice,
No anger, no rage, no ego, no game
Used as negative device,
We share our dream laid before our eyes
So the flame never dies
Together we rise and stay,
Lyrically justified.

IDENTITY
(Legacy/Following your heart/Inner strength)

SOUL SPRIT

By Empress Imani

Soul spirit, I see you...
Wishing that your old price tags were brand new
Looking in the mirror asking who is the reflection you see?
Masked in memories of what use to be
kaleidoscoped between coloured dreams and nightmares
Cold, unexplained Stares, believing you're damaged beyond
repair, with a broken smile you stick together with super glue
every single morning...

Through every trial, you bask in self-denial,
Gripped by the expectations of your inner child.
I am here to tell you to stop shrinking
Try listening and not over thinking
Look closely without blinking for the vision is crystal clear
What you require shall soon appear
And even when it does I'll still be here.

Injecting a concoction of consciousness and confidence into
the centre of your soul,
And while you absorb in the essence, you fight evanescence,
feel your ancestors' presence
It's grounding, with heart pounding
Embrace it
This is your time to face it, there is nothing else in this world to
replace it, a foundation so strong that nothing can shake it.
Your own sanctuary depends on the conditions of what
extends beyond your auric field
Be aware you're not healed, and that the universe still has

many things to reveal.

Masked by echoes of your former self,
Trying to scream its way into existence, with utter persistence,
Met constantly with hints of resistance,
Every time you attempt to move forward,
Just a few steps towards the light, in hopes to reignite,
Whatever it is inside of you that may have died.

I'm telling you to be still for a moment and rest your mind,
Then for the first time tap into within,
Shed your skin, and as your chakras align,
Really open wide your third eye, for you are eternally
permitted to rise,
Do what's right for the spirit with no compromise
I see the liquid gold trickling inside of you
I see the parts of you that easily bruise
I see the you that lay weary and confused
The marks left from constant patterns of abuse,
And beneath the cracks, running up the spine in your back, is
your passion, your desire and your kundalini fire.

You are bursting to become a master of your very own
destiny,
To be a new version of what it really means to be free.
Forming new definitions while finding your feet
Turning up the volume with which you speak.
So you can then speak volumes to the ears of the weak...
Soul spirit I see you...
Old soul but brand new, recognised by a few.
I see you.

PIED PIPER

By Denetta D3 Copeland

Amazing... Creative,
A feeling sits within me
Native
Abrasive, Paraphrasing...
Anything to keep me from vegetative states
I try to stay awake,
I fight for goodness sake,
Crazy life's so evasive,
Try not to make mistakes,
No sight...
And no-ones waiting
I cry,
But you're...
Sedated.

Please don't follow the Pied Piper
Follow in my shoes,
There's so much more code to decipher
Don't listen to his tune,
Cover your ears and close your eyes
You'll see so much more from inside you
Conquer your fears...
See through the disguise
We have nothing left to loose.

Hiatus manipulative
Praising anything that's been advocated
Captivated... Fascinated,

History prefabricated,
Wait!
Try give your head a shake,
However long it takes,
Don't stop 'till your whole body aches
The future is opaque.
Frustrating,
Educated - tonight is your assassination.

Please don't follow the Pied Piper, follow in my shoes,
There's so much more code to decipher, don't listen to his
tune.
Cover your ears and close your eyes,
You'll see so much more from inside you,
Conquer your fears,
See through the disguise
We have nothing left to loose.

I'm wasted, that's basic
Scrunching up my face from what I just tasted
Intricated, covering all bases,
Painting your canvass, leaving you no traces...
Desolate
So now we're human bait,
Make way for super states,
Shall we just embrace it?
It's someone else's fate,
Looks like we're human fakes
Walking around in perfect figures of eight.

Please don't follow the Pied Piper, follow in my shoes,
There's so much more code to decipher, don't listen to his
tune.

Cover your ears and close your eyes,
You'll see so much more from inside you.
Conquer your fears, see through the disguise
We have nothing left to loose.

Dominated, Aggravated,
Holding all the bloody aces
Procrastinated, Intoxicated,
Society is putting me through my paces
Relate?
I can accept my fate,
I know I must keep faith
Hope my time ain't wasted,
Just trying to penetrate
You can't out run the human race,
It just keeps chasing.

Please don't follow the Pied Piper, follow in my shoes,
There's so much more code to decipher, don't listen to his
tune,
Cover your ears and close your eyes,
You'll see so much more from inside you,
Conquer your fears,
See through the disguise
We have nothing left to loose.

MY GRANDAD

By Saju Ahmed

On the streets of Leeds is where I want to be
Memoirs of immigrant engraved on the tarmac
Windows singing in reggae rhythms, Bollywood ballets
Chapeltown, dancing in the summer sun.

Granddad stood over me like tower blocks
Shading me from temptation
While conversation sound like spitfire twist of tongues
Grown men move hands while painting their stories.

Chasing after horses, was the money making option
These dark skinned men didn't speak English like my teachers
But broken as the system that brought them here.

My granddad clapped hands in conversations
Gripped palms with men from islands he has never seen before
They called him Miah so he would never forget his father
Never forget, you Bengali boy traded your silk lungi
For a suit that fits right, tight as the freedom fighter
fist handing on to life.

My granddad always dreamed, laughed, smiled
For the race he carried on his back
Smooth enough to have white women in his presence
While he was too dark for the union jack.

My granddad prayed 5 times a day
Married 3 women, sweated his youth any in factories

Travelled up and down the spine of this land
Fought 2 wars, he saw the birth of Bangladesh, the rise of the
national fronts
Strength of a seaman sons to see it through alone in the
sixties.

My granddad will always remind me
Of the stretch of summer, 90s Leeds
The corners he once stood painting stories with his hands
I smile writing this…

I find myself doing the same things, on the same corner
With men whose granddads came from islands
That I've never seen before
My granddad is the man I'm slowly becoming.

WORDS OF SELF-CONSTRUCTION

By Nadinne Dyen

You're not my architect,
No matter how much you try to draw my plans,
Your technical knowledge,
Intricate designs, use qualifications to undermine,
I'm under construction,
Progress in development,
Not a development opportunity for you to seize,
Without consent using my keys,
Attempting to impose my interior,
You're inferior,
I am my own architect,
God and I's hands that create
My master plans, in which I take my commands,
I'm legally protected property,
For only I choose to whom I open the door,
Your calculations,
Twisted manifestations,
Mathematical equations,
Will never manipulate me,
After many reconstructions,
I'm not going to be losing myself easily,
Giving myself freely,
I'm not for sale, you can't buy me,
No settlement for joint ownership,
Check my contract,
Golden script,
Your dictatorship serves no purpose,
I'm not a projection of your own worthlessness,
Your army of artisans,

Stone masons and carpenters, are valueless
As the draught is already sketched,
Blueprints already etched,
For this construction is now my home,
I am finally, Blissfully, Ever blessed

You are not my composer ... I compose myself,
As much as view me as the staff lines on which you feel you
can smoothly place your musical notes,
Sadly you do not have enough beats to fulfil the notes in
which my heart pulsates,
Oscillates,
Although I can choice-fully swing in the timing of the scales of
MAAT,
To view the duality if all things,
My natural rhythm beats passionately ... Rapidly,
Yes, Humbly I can be,
But, Yes I am in search for innovative solutions,
You would convince me I was trapped by my own
impatience,
Blind to this passion and deep love towards the universe,
You would always jump on my verse,
You would curse,
I had an inability to rise,
Or was I actually limited to the confinements of my
surroundings,
Boundless beats of my heart,
Impatient to full fill my purpose,
Is my impatience really a burden?
Or patience a need I need to be learning?
Or perhaps there's a need so harrowing that my impatience is
my passion,
A reaction to the tears that I see falling?

See, I'm in tempo …
As much as you can slow me down, I'm not a victim to your rebound,
You can't speed me up, To push me into a relationship,
See I got my own pace, And I'm Deeper then Sir Coxsone's bass

I'm not your instrument,
You can't play me, fiddle me, beat me,
Or provocatively tweak me,
I'm an instrument of JAH … Yeah, that can sometimes play out of tune,
But generally sounding sweetly, Harmoniously,
To my own Symphony,
State of Grace, able to hold my own space,
Fearless of my own company,
Or to stand alone, in acapella I rhyme,
Taking down the walls of Jericho,
Sharing my heart with reverbs and echoes

Your hands cannot sculpt me,
Slide down my curves,
Repetitive strokes to shape my waistline,
Wetting your hands to moistly model my thighs,
Cupping my breasts to the image you wished sized,
Flattened, pointed, lifted, enlarged to your desire,
This control is sickening,
Getting you off,
Making you higher,
Modelling your delusions,
Finishing me off in the fire,
You're not the potter that creates me,

I'm on the wheel of creation,
Circle of life,
That hand Khnum spins,
Infused with the breath if the divine, Sublime,
Actualizing me as a unique vessel,
Individual and special,
A vessel that fire can no longer break,
Forsake,
Visible mantle crusts,
Like the earth plates,
Unhidden cracks,
Lay upon my surface,
Once wounds softer then oil,
Merciful lines,
In the body of my vase are the scars,
The trails if my stories,
History of my ruptures,
Congruence of my repairs,
Transformations,
Improvements of the times laid bare,
This container is strong,
My purpose virtuous,
Not for you to pour,
Transfer,
Your flood of insecurities into me,
I'm not your insecurities,
I am not what you want me to be, not all you think that I am,
I'm not here to fulfil your ever need,
I'm not here to make you solely valued,
I'm not your victim,
I'm not your abandoned pier, I'm not the pier you sail back too,
I'm not here to be rescued,

I'm not here to be your rescuer,
I am not only sex,
I'm not just your fantasy,
I am not your blank screen in which you project your own cruelties,
And make me believe I am them,
I am not your mental insanity,
I am not your absence without leave,
I'm not all you believe, not all you perceive,
That you grieve,
And I'm certainly not the only love that you can receive.

THE COUNTRYMAN RETURNS

By SilverFinger Singh

I'm So Sick Of These People Tryna Bring A SINGH Down.
As I Speak The Truth, I See You Smiling Through Your Frown.

As I Step Onto The Stage, I Be Reppin' With My Crown.
I'm A Lion With My Maine, I Be Feeling So Proud.

Who Provides For The Pride Even If The Waters Dried?
As The Two Worlds Collide, There's No Where To Hide!

In This Time Of Now?! We've Had To Allow.
The Violence And Criminals.. It's Very Visible.

It Pivotal, You Know This Message Ain't Subliminal.

It's Pitiful, How We Live?! - Its A Miracle.

You Know It's Difficult.

I'm Working To Pay Bills, Is This Liveable?

People Giving Up And Living So Miserable.

You Know The Country-Man Survives, Through The Heart Ache
and Lies,
This Hunger For Success Dries A Tear In My Eye.

I'm Wading In The Water, Pushed Away By The Tide.
Walking Through The Backstreet As I Ponder To Decide,
Whilst Taken For A Ride.

I Meditate And Vibe, With Blessings From My Satguru
Everything Is Alright.

IT'S REAL

By Princess Emmanuelle (EmpresS *1)

No fake lashes,
No fake eyebrows,
No fake nails,
No fake lips, bust or butt,
Currently No fake hair.
No fake eye contacts,
No tattoos or poison to ma blood.
No extra piercings,
No liposuction, fade out creams, relaxers, or fake
transformations as such.
No meat, no fizzy, no chems,
No intoxicating products,
Not 4me, Nah none of dem!

Real eyelashes,
Real eyebrows,
Real nails,
Real lips, bust 'n butt,
Real hair.
Real eyes,
Real nose,
Real skin,
Real heart,
Real Soul Love From within x
All natural,
All healthy Everytin',
Organically rooted and pure juz like my feelings.
Don't do or say a thing unless I mean it,
So deep and genuine U can feel it.
Blind urself 2da physikal da material,
Talk to others thru the heart Thru the Spirit,
So deep and genuine U can feel it.
Like a Mama's instinctive love 4her baby.

It's so Real, It is so Real,
I'm da Raw deal, I'm da Real deal,
As God created me.

PLACE OF FREEDOM

HOPE

By Steve Duncan

There's a song in our souls that sings for more
And its chorus is full of hope.
It is the treatment of all spiritual sickness
But never the cure
Hope
Regardless of the present situation
Through the interchangeable phases of our lives
We are all defied at times by that one liner,
That elusive quotation.
The one that defines all universal language,
The one that, without which, all other virtues would never exist.
It's constantly defended by faith and courage.
The one that typifies and signifies
The underlying message of all spiritual notes.
Hope
Let me break it down for you!
Hope
H-O-P-E
Happy other people exist

Hope
H-O-P-E
Harnessing other people's Experiences
Positive and negative
Hope
H-O-P-E
Having open perception to Education

So you can learn from it.
Hope

If at any time you're struggling to remember
Hope is
H-O-P-E
That halo over promised Emancipation.
Regardless of the situation.
Keep on persevering,
You will see Hope become a tangible reality.
You will feel hope
H-O-P-E
Hearty Old processes Ended
HOPE HOPE HOPE
I'm gonna ram it down your throat
Until you're sick of it.
Until it cuts your insides and starts to bleed your insecurities.
Until it seeps into your skin and begins to define You.
Till the sky is never too high for you to soar through.
It's proper propaganda to believe
You should never have your head in the clouds
Cos we were born to stand out
To get higher and higher
Deeper and deeper and more philosophical.

Hope is the antidote
To suppressing your perception of the possible.
Cos hope loves You, You, You,
With all your warts and all your flaws
And all these rules, and all these laws.
God doesn't make mistakes
He just made you in a way
Where you can learn from yours.

Cos hope means no-ones beyond redemption
Everybody's got a dignity
that needs to be affirmed
With the correct attention.
Cos hope exists for this very reason
To weather the storms and the rainy seasons.

So no matter how far down the scale you go
I want you to know
that this Poem is with you.
Cos we've all got grace
We've all got scope
If no-matter what happens
We just be willing
to just keep clinging to
HOPE

FREEDOM ROAD

By Idren Natural aka I-n-I oneness

"Excuse me sir, I am lost, can you help me get to freedom road please?"

Most certainly brother, come with me...

We shall make a stop on Equality Street
There are so many nice people we shall meet
Then we forward up Justice Avenue
Meet more people so humble and true.
Then we see a round-a-bout
People, people, don't have no doubt,
Forward ever, backward never,
Forward ever, backward never...
We're going to freedom road.

We reach the place - Love Way
Have to move, all of the way
When we reach to the top
We hold a stop
Hold a juice from the Ital shop
We're going to freedom road.

We'll see the traffic lights,
Red, gold and green
It's a Rasta man scene,
Do you know what I mean?
Hills and valleys
Beautiful country

We're going to freedom road.

We reach the place called Harmony Hill
Where everything is cool, calm and still
When we reach the top, we hold another break
Eat a slice of Ital cake
We're going to freedom road

When we reach down the hill we'll see a bungalow
Inside the bungalow lives Bongo Joe
If you ask him right, he'll tell you where to go
But before we go!
We must sip a cup,
Read a psalm from Jah holy book,
JAH GUIDANCE along the way
F R E E D O M ROAD...

THE CITY SONG

By Testament

This is the place where I sleepwalk, then I wake again
A strange home that its residents are strangers in
It's always on the move but it never speaks
And if you never been, I guess you'll never quite get it
The City. The rhythm I'm in step with
Where high-rise kids see with bird's eye perspective
Next to suburbs that they're not connected with
And best mind the gap, cos there lurks the nemesis
We're stuck in boxes like scientific specimens
Working for different ends, but the same city stresses
It's like the smog's an anesthetic
As if we're so afraid to catch something, we forget to catch
the message
But don't catch eyes on the pavement where you treading
Cos matters too pressing to sympathize with the street
dwellings
And the smell of it, catches me off guard,
Still I offer a few pennies cos times are hard
I try and ask some questions, get down to brass tacks
I'm like: "Where's your family, mate?" He just laughs back
Honestly, I can't grasp that, but that's the city way
You see trouble just walk at a quicker pace
Cos mankind's got bad credit,
Living by a precipice where adverts are prevalent
Saying: "Be careful who you're friendly with"
And now everybody's scared, because we all terrorists
But I see between the decadent and derelict
The heritage and heretic

The self-made man and the self-made menace
Manufactured with a mindset like manic depressive
It's the City...

Where you work, where you eat
Where you hide, where you meet
Where you cry, where you weep
It's the City...

Where you wake, where you sleep
Where you fall, where you reach
Where you're trapped, where you're free
It's the City...

In this City... full of freaks at night they emerge
Streets fade to orange light falls on the curb
I murmur something ...I can't hear myself think above the
Sound of traffic, the City's percussion
As we kick against the snare, snare against the kick,
Meet brares dealing wares on concrete stairs
The case, they plead theirs...
But only God can free them, that's why I'm writing these
street prayers
Cos funny things, happen on the way to the forum
Where someone's story is unexpectedly shortened
They cordon off the area, youths stay dawdling
Ignoring the causes of why the rich stay fortunate
Cos fortune made the city, money built the premises
Promised we'd make it, but then hid all the entrances
Trying to sky scrape takes sterling effort
The City work ethic, will kill you if you let it

Pedestrians look lifeless

My head's bowed like a Lowry lifework
Inner City Life: like its Timeless
My Heart-beat, between the silence and the sirens
Migrants facing the racist violence, ignorant mindsets
While kids make strangers visit the off license

From the highest point wisdom and folly are calling
And Plod keep plodding like they forgotten Stephen
Lawrence

In the Rush Hour, you're quicker walking
It's Two-thou and *still* slums house city orphans
Acid rain falls-on, both richest and the poorest
Closed Circuit cameras got us all recorded
Another day ends, in this place I was created in
Where different cultures, faces mix and blend
A love-hate relationship, things keep changing it,
No mistaking it, it's the people that make it....

In the City...
Where you work, where you eat
Where you hide, where you meet
Where you cry, where you weep
It's the City...

Where you wake, where you sleep
Where you fall, where you reach
Where you're trapped, where you're free
It's the City...

FREE AS CAN BE

By Shaun Clarke aka Shaun MC

Bewilder me with your madness
Stump me with silliness
Arrest me for your self-preservation
Taunt me with your sense of superiority,
Provoke me with ignorance,
Stupefy me with Saturnism,
Confuse me with misguidance,
Stress me with idiocy,
Then let me be...

Caught me on your web since when I remember
I know no other home
Had me in a village with walls,
Drip fed me so I could live,
But couldn't dig a tunnel out.
Rock me with wickedness
Sink me with selfishness
Budge me while in a rush to keep up with the Joneses
Punish me indirectly, in secrecy
Hidden in plain sight
Politically correct me to close me down
Worry me with your woes,
Then leave me be...

Smile on me like a friend,
Like an innocent party,
As if we are all in the same boat

As if we're all to stay afloat
You spun a web for the money
To pay your way
To feed your family,
Regardless of indirect consequences
The negative, deadly impact on others,
Like a being out of date,
You fail to make the connection
Never programmed that way.

Tell you what!
I'll try to reciprocate if you...

Impress me with your depth
Amuse me with your humour
Nudge me with good news
Please me with your positivity
Delight me with your wisdom
Hold me with your worthy advice
Praise me for my bravery
Respect me for being reasonable
Console me with consideration
Then come and see me again sometime...

Reach me with friendship
Cover me in peace and politeness
Smile with genuine good intention
From the heart, not as an actor
Submit to admission
That we are equally exclusive
Mutually dependant
Treat me with acknowledgement,
Show me truth and nobility

Respect my dignity
Then prove it, so that I can judge you.
Then allow me to reply without pressure or manipulation
Question subconscious conditioning.

If only I'd been given, or even noticed that chance to
develop my wings
I know nothing else, nothing but the web
And I'm stuck in the muck of it
Tired from the struggling
Worn from the battles.
I'm prepared since predestined to die,
Caught out by the unknown,
The unexpected.

So... go ahead,

Mislead me with your lies and pride
Dumb me down with denial
Kick me with your deception
Hit me with your blissfulness
Shoot me with your gun
Blow me with your bombs
Blind me with your sun shiny shallowness,
And please wait a moment!
Have you heard about The Freedom Project?
Nuff respect!
Sounds right up my street.

Meet me half way with mutual respect
If not, won't you Self reflect
Set me free, as a bird should be
I'm not trying to be absurd

I dare you, c'mon...
Arm me with knowledge
So I'm free to make my choice
From mind control
Set me as free - as can be.

UNTIL MY FLESH DIES

By Justin Swaby aka Wordgineer

When lives looking low, I look up at the stars and I know there's hope
Hope to live, hope to love, hope to grow.
So I hold on another day to battle on and I pray the Lord guides me along the way
So I can stay out of the clutches of darkness in my heart I feel that he harkens
Sent me as sheep, secret assignment, wolves laying traps behind me
In the city of rats, foxes and cats
All dark little love nil-grats hard to view where you're at
Like an Ostrich in a sandbag, many reach for the gat busting caps
Bloody heads splat on the pavement, red craven
Let the devil in and he'll blame you, flame you then switch face to shame you
Led into temptation like able we are able time to turn tables we are able
Love is waiting faithful with help from angels
Stars life and creation too beautiful for him to create so the Devil tempts away to destroy things
Sending his demons in weak moments to women, men and children
Halting life is only missioning.......
Create division check his system divide, rule and conquer
Can only work with no exposure

Get the picture paper read all about it!
No sense to doubt it, growing up rowdy, should it be this way

No way! Youth should be playing life's game not aiming to
take it away
Yet past leaders make it ok to be this way
Still I pray for change have time to rearrange
The worlds stage from heading to rage
Through time releasing the blame
Motivation required when life's looking dim
Have a favourite song to sing, then in a whim of a whimsical
You realise that when you point there's three pointing back
at you
Wondering screwed tight shut onto your head like a nut
Belt and brace for taste, dressed for the occasion.

Two faced hypocrite or experienced rich play
Not wanting to turn away, dark decay, flesh stays
Soul embargo onward home, here to roam free
Not in shackled slavery of economic or any kind
Many enriching one life, more for one to enrich many
Like 99+1 copper to gold penny
When it drops self-adornment too much
Sky fly bluff like coat fluff, sticky tape away
Cleansed to stay rather soul over material to display
Made to shine, grow and rise
In bed dream deep into mind
Take your time, rush often leads to hasty haze
Eye's unseen like flatulence waste, yet some still choose to
walk that way
Empty, such a crying shame.

Much more than this Legacy to stay
Remain once in heaven sourced palace of 12 gates
Returning home smiling face, thinking may have slipped
dusted off tried again

Praise, Praised and give thanks
Most high working magic via Holy Ghost
Prophesied scripture sent to grip us through the thorny path
valley full of the shadows of death
Only the cat was killed because of curiosity.

Story of caution to heed once bitten then twice shy soul food
to feed
Good thoughts bear good deeds, seen to believe
Untrusting to unknown, blowing caution to the wind
Not truly wise idea, better to step with care
Living each day as it's your last saving thought for tomorrow
Leaving past sorrows borrowed.

(Deep Breath)
Breath in the nectar of life, worry not just additional strife
Relax unwind the mind give love the room to thrive
Full cup spills each try, overflowing into others the Ying and
Yang among us
The net that bonds thus as we hurt another we hurt ourselves
Shelved for eternal, internal web, ebb the flow, fresh show
Happy to know, force higher then earth guiding yet not
infringing free-will
Still the situation not out of hand on this our promised land of
a globe
It's to share our glorious home, how many other places like
earth do we know
Yet content on destroy it so though I may be all alone with
these thoughts in mind
I'll share these thoughts with my pen
Please let's stop these inhumane fights,
These words I write until my flesh dies.

P.E.A.C.E

By Saiqa Rehman aka Lightening Sykes

When I look inside myself, I feel the peace.
When I look around me, I see chaos on the streets.
Souls are lost, people forget to breathe,
Minds occupied with no time to dream.
If I could make a difference
I'd use the figure of speech,
Stand alone with no fear to speak what's on my mind.
Speak in a rhythmic beat,
Write it out crystal clear and spell out;
P.e.a.c.e.

Peace is at hand,
Close, in your hands,
Reach within the peace that would beat in your hands,
An emotion of stillness,
Breathing so shallow
With rays of peace casting over all shadows.

If I could give everyone peace of mind,
Give you hope and faith,
Would you break it as bread,
If compassion was felt?
Would we see blood shed
Stand around watching the dead?

What has this world become?
At times feeling as though
I hate this place, I feel disgraced,
How societies ignorant with its ways,
I'd break the chain.

In the roles being played,
Untie the blindfold in the game
And take the stakes,
Die as innocent as my first day.
There is no blood on my hand,
No premeditated plan.
I've had enough of the clans
That take from the lands.
Man's destroyed the land
We need to fix up and give a helping hand;
P.e.a.c.e.

Now if every time the tide moves,
Would it bring the peace,
Rippling waves across oceans and seas,
Ships full off essential and necessity,
Cracking down poverty,
No homeless on the streets,
No third world poverty,
We're all one, can't you see?
Has the world gone crazy, or is it just me?
Am I too sensitive?
Or am I climbing up the wrong tree?
Born in the wrong era?

I hear a soul scream,
If love has been found,
Then peace is the crown,
Wearing it proud,
With no judgement that clouds,
The feeling in my heart,
Is spelling peace out loud;
P.e.a.c.e

FREEDOM

Karabo Moruakgomo
aka By Kayb

Walkin in the streets like a man on a mission
Man in the mirror can't even see his own reflection
Identity crisis, to you, freedom is just an expression
Cos' you live through their acceptance
And die from their rejection

Trying to reach out to your roots,
but failed to make the connection
If it's because of your complexion,
doesn't mean you can't be accepted
You're out there seeking for freedom,
but people lead you the wrong direction,
Trying to make it to a free world,
but can't make it to the next election

Freedom's barrier is the chains and shackles on your wrists
and feet
With the 'masters' hand over your mouth,
Taking ur freedom of speech
Children stripped from their childhood
and forced to work in the streets
Dom in freedom, meaning dominant, and I demand them to
be free

Freedom on your face, meaning your happy and smiling
No feeling of violence,
And no tape on your lips to alter your silence

If freedom is a feeling, then it ain't a feeling that we been
feeling before
Cos' I express my freedom, pain and struggle
I'm free from it all

Freedom and responsibility will end this cancer of poverty
Cos' freedom in a child will give them a heart filled with purity

Freedom is what we're here for,
What we live for,
What we cry for,
and what we die for
Stand up for something and live for anything
Or stand up for nothing and fall for everything

Freedom is never earned,
It is always demanded
I fight for freedom
knowing hope and faith are my companions
I long for freedom even though I am short of time
I longed for peace way before I wrote my rhymes

I live in peace and acceptance,
What our hearts beat for
So take off the chains and shackles
And demand for your freedom

REFLEXIONS
(Heroes & Villains)

DEAR NANA

By Axsom Nelson

This one's for my Nana…
Rest in peace Nana,
I know you're up in heaven
Smiling down with your brethren
I think about you 24/7
Past away, and you left a depression
And that's the reason I'm stressing
Getting weeded, I'm needing a blessing.

In the game, ducking one time,
I see pain when I look in my mum's eyes,
Just know your son tries
Just know one day they'll be sunshine
Dear Nana we miss you, so much tears not enough tissue
I remember life was blissful,
You here, making flames in the kitchen,
You, here, would of gave me conviction.

Dear Nana,
I know you're with me
On my journey
Please forgive me for being unruly
If I don't do them first, they will do me,
I can't hold my head down when they screw me
If I don't do them first, they will do me.
I remember what you taught me,
Don't come back home if they short me.
Got stick from the racist Ice scream man

So you came back and smashed up the ice-cream van
Rest in peace, Valerie Icyling Clarke
Forever, you got my heart
We can never break apart
Now I cherish all I have,
Hoping that it lasts,
Promise that I'll play my part,
Bringing light into dark.

Yours Faithfully, Axsom

LADY LIBERTY

By Edson Burton

Listless she wanders in rags
Sewn from rainbow flags
Peeling from flint shoulders
Her hem trails in treacle thick
Foul waters coursing down gutters.

Her name bartered and sold
Turn marble tongues to gold.
Day-glow prizes take the eye
Away from her unadorned promise.

Denied access to the banquet
Held daily in her honour
She slips quite as mist into myth.
On the street a silent throng
holding vigil remember waiting
Waiting.

A-YO, NELSON

By Saju Ahmed

A-yo, Nelson, did you hear them?
A-yo, Nelson, did you see them?
A-yo, Mr Mandela, don't believe in the tears they cry
for you
They hated you first, loved you last…
And still want death to us.

The music, the chains made while strangling your
hands ankles
They danced and cracked smiles like the rocks on
Robben Island,
U can hear the grit of their teeth sounds like greed is
bleeding in their gums
They knew this melody would play for life.

They tell me you are a terrorist; you wanted tear
apart the apartheid
Modern day Moses apart the tied coming with force
You envisioned through muddy waters the long
distance
My captain…feels like going home - The country boy
knows
The feeling cold weather blues. After the rain hurting
souls
Screamin' and crying rambling minds, lost like
ancestor bottom of the sea
Fathers and sons standing round crying,
I'm ready to clash with jealous hearted men.

They said you spread wickedness like disease of the
white man in South Africa
They didn't know you was the cure, you was
freedom,
You are the lonely man blues, sang by a nation
You can't escape the blues but it's alright.

You waged war with the weight they left on your
shoulders
They told me slavery ended 1833, but forgot to free
you the people
The Same Thing is still going on sex trade, servants,
forced labour, child labour
They say your brothers in arms were monster Gadhafi,
Castro, Arafat
I salute you with the trumpet of blues, 'cos we are in
mourning
To me you are a Hero, your brothers are supermen
Been a king, (Ben E king,) the beginning of it all
Only you know and I Know, All of your tomorrows.

The white moon rises in the darkness
Oppressed by the people who sell freedom as
democracy
I thought we had a right to stand up for our rights
Stand up for our beliefs just as you did.

So I guess democracy is when demons crossed the
sea
Hypocrites tell us we are in the wrong for fighting
back
When they've creased the link for thousands of years,

When they held the guns to the mouths of our
mothers
The burning English bullet engraved on our tongues
I sit and wonder what this world will be like if you
wasn't caged
Like an animal… would Africa become a power
house?
With you and Gadhafi using your own satellite…
raising back to greatest
Would Palestine be Palestine without the Israeli and
American Invasion?
Would the Middle East be on fire? You sir are a true
leader
Not afraid to fight, not afraid to forgive, not afraid to
talk, not afraid to die
And today you are free for real.

A-yo, Nelson, did you hear them?
A-yo, Nelson, did you see them?
A-yo, Mr Mandela, don't believe in the tears they cry
for you
They hated you first - Loved you last…
And still want death to us.

TOMORROW STARTS TODAY

By Denetta D3 Copeland

So there goes the day
You decide to leave
Though I hope and pray
I do not succeed
You don't wanna stay cosy here with me
I should not invade this space that you need.

I might be broken, and it may ache
But I'll never let you take my heart away
It's not a token, or a keepsake
Forever is over, Tomorrow starts today.

Boy I am amazed
You wanna be free
I am left afraid
How will I proceed?
Life is in a daze
I can barely breathe
While you just play
With your latest squeeze.

I might be broken, and it may ache
But I'll never let you take my heart away
It's not a token, or a keepsake
Forever is over, Tomorrow starts today.

It's more than I can take
You just watch me bleed

I am lost in grey
Bring sunlight please
You are all I crave
So now you're just a tease
You say I will be ok
'Cos that's what you believe.

I might be broken, and it may ache
But I'll never let you take my heart away
It's not a token, or a keepsake
Forever is over, Tomorrow starts today.

PERFUME

By Testament

Hey, it's not over yet
So she told me she was alone in a mess
Broke and in debt,
No comfort zone
Just zoned out and depressed
I told her the days not done till the sun goes to rest

Don't use these words for poetic effect
Words heard are perfume
See they can pick up the scent
So she can pick herself up again
See every day's a little attempt
To move from the fray to the fragrant
The fifth sense

Aromatherapy for the soul
Let God, let go
Inhale it deep
Breathe in the nose
Out through the mouth
Downward we drown
In sweet incense
What I speak of is spiritual
The Spirit falls
Falling slowly

Only in a sense this incense forms a sentence
The poetry of perfume

And she a pearl who was lost
Or an alabaster box broken
For a parable, the purpose we never knew
Until we saw her smile burst through
Melodies
Fragrance
Breathe in her aura like
Perfume

VIBRATIONS
(Attitude and influence)

TIME SUSPENDED

By Princess Emmanuelle (EmpresS *1)

I wanna talk about Society...
I wanna talk about Morality...
Wanna discuss class, material, and Immortality.
At a time when you could just look to a person and
have a conversation without speech.
When you could think and act what you thought,
and know it would be respected as it is real...ism,
and I wanna deliver to you these 'isms',
To me it is a mission I aim to complete.
Wanna tell you it all,
just need your peace, openess and respect, for me
to release...
So if you increase your engagement,
realise your potential,
to inspirational attention.
Then I would like to behold you in an angle,
a point of reflection,
and I don't have to mention,
to you what you don't understand.
-'Cause you do.
You just always gotta' remember what we already
know,
to undo the dream that we are caught-up in.
So we as a Nation can Overstand, Unite, and
Begin,...
To really live, act upon, then tell of this story that we
are in.

...When the time arrives,
When we are here awaiting,
When the time reaches a Worldwide standstill and
no-one is explaining.
When it is difficult to believe the very source of
Reality,
When what is occurring is labelled as 'Mysticality'.
When the information that has been force-fed into
our brains
becomes the very reality of lie.
Misguidance is the Scientific cry.
But why do we continue to believe and buy?
Why stop asking 'Why?'

'Cause we're on the path of Immortality,
where every uncertainty directs to the so-called
'reality'.
Every cry for guidance and actions of denying the
material shouldn't be called 'insanity'.
Where you begin to question, to form your opinion,
And the 'your', the 'you', the 'individual',
Don't have to keep quite and keep sitting...
In the seat of denial to the self.
The seat that will not help you to help yourself.
The seat that don't 'llow you to pray out loud and
give peaceful blessings,
unless your saying your vows!

But do not worry my beautiful people,
'cause the time I speak of is soon coming.
It will surprise the scene, and every bein'.
Every bein' that hasn't been, to the time I'm talking
in.

KING OF DREADS

By Saju Ahmed

He is the King of Dreads
Locking philosophies in the mind of the wanderers
Strumming his whole life beyond guitar strings, *"The Wailing wailer"*
"Hurts to be alone," but *"one love" is* all we need
"Simmer down" before one hit cracks, dead your heart with cold
"Lonesome felling" hangs with *"Rude boys"* like Ackee from the island trees
Swaying side to side like the Rasta's, the trench town souls
Whose feet are battered with blues rhythm in the bones.

He is the Lion of Judah
"Soul Rebel" created *in the womb of tribe of joseph*
Exiled driven to forget *memoirs* of great grandmother olden time stories
"It's Alright" "The Cornerstone" the builder refused
Built the house for ones with no shoes
Sang songs with messages of *"400 years"* of the same oppression
His imagination was covered in white silk... He the Calf of the movement
If cut then we the people can't walk... so his heart bleed onto hymns
Reasoning through the mystic clouds of Ganja. Vision of *"Dreamland"*

Where *"The Sun is shining"* fist full of melodies
changed Rhodesia to Zimbabwe
But we still "*Stand alone"* but never forgot to "*Get up,
Stand up" The Burnin*
Won't stop cause *"Them Belly Full"* but we still hungry.

He is the Rebel of music
"No Woman, no cry" "So Jah She," the *"Natty Dread"*
Will bring" *Revolution," so" Bend down low"*
Grab your courage with your tongue, you "*have so
much things to say"*
In the" *misty morning" "Crisis"* cries the loudest "*Time
will tell"*
*"Is this love" "Coming in from the cold" "Smile
Jamaica..."*
"Zion train" has dragged itself to your station
Redemption came through song, finally "*could you
be loved"*
By the *"Stiff necked fools"   "give thanks and praises"*
"I know"" Rasta man live up" Trench town CHEER UP
*As the king of dread gave you victory
R.I.P Bob Marley.*

NO BAD VIBES

By David Okwesia
aka Full Flava

No Bad Vibes
We're in the no war zone
Zonked on a cone
Not alone, moving strong like a falling stone
From a mountain top dar gon gon style
Wicked and a wild
Drop nonstop to the top
So if you can't cope with the dope note, don't choke
on your throat
Take it easy, step aside as we rock your socks with the
hip hop reggae vibes
Make you shock, make you shock.

Paint pictures, fixtures for Italness
No bad vibes, but consciousness
Paint pictures, fixtures for Italness
No bad vibes, but consciousness,

Dread to whatever snake skin shiver
Shudder, I give thanks to my mother
I born to deliver some bawl inna-ragga hip-hop
stylee.

Paint pictures, fixtures for Italness
No bad vibes, just consciousness
Paint pictures, fixtures for Italness
No bad vibes, just consciousness,

Feelings frustrations floating, can't hold back
Seasons change
'Nuff tings a-gwarn in mad head, reasons why my
hair turn to dread
Winner, like Yell Brinner fanciness, no fancy dress
A rise, no disguise, I'm the Star of David, never to be
faded my mind strength, Heaven sent
Rub into the future, you can erase it, who schools
yeah
Laws of the system
Class room teacher don't greet ya with any of our
history
Over shadowed truth without proof, so my mind don't
reach.

Paint pictures, fixtures for Italness
No bad vibes, pure consciousness
Paint pictures, fixtures for Italness
No bad vibes, just consciousness

HAPPINESS

By Axsom Nelson

Every individual has their own outlook on life
The one thing we all have in common is reality
No one can deny the fact of gravity,
Or the fact that we live in a world full of anarchy.
We can try to hide from the tragedy,
But at the end of the day,
We still have to bow down to her majesty.
Every day we seek clarity,
Because we just want to live happily.

All I see is vanity
She missed the sales so she's panicking
Sometimes even if just for a moment
I lose sanity.
We're always trying to be accepted by someone
else,
When the truth is;
People only care about themselves.

I say, who cares
We've made it through the worst
The curse of money makes us forget
To put our families first.

Like what is more important, time spent or time lost?
In a world where everybody wants to be the boss
It's a fight to get your point across
Where is the love? I ask, and look above to the skies

hoping someone hear my cries.
And someone notices my drive
Only then I'll be buzzing in this hive.

Just the other day
I read something on Instagram that I felt
It was a meme that read; '*happiness is a personal thing and it really doesn't have nothing to do with anyone else*'
Yes indeed this meme put a smile on my face
Gave me motivation to run in this race,
And just in case I lose my place,
Remember where there's a will, there's a way.

FOOLISH LOVE

By Shamile Haline

When will they stop?
A million phones she forgot
Now I hunt your love
We could have been one.

Run, run, run,
My foolish love
Run, run, run,

Memories are still young
Forgetting you is like forgetting myself
Love that's one way feels like hell
Cry over you, though it's the end.

Run, run, run,
My foolish love
Run, run, run,

My foolish love.

INTO PERSPECTIVE
(Ways of seeing)

THE ZONES

By J Bravo

The Zones, hostels, foster homes…
Bull keep harassing us on the way home
Beef still fresh - You should've stayed home tonight
Instead of dying for your pride, have foresight
Dying for her? She's a mess and a bag-head,
Breeding up who should've been a one-time
shagging
You asked for trouble, see Deebo loves Feleicia
You probably couldn't tell 'cos he regularly beats her,
But he funds her skunk habit.

Some Skets you should turn down, frontline man don't
touch what they own
Watch 'em park up in the Audi kitted out nice, once
they harvest cash money from the fast life
Get gripped? Earn 18 grand for five years, 'Keep your
mouth shut!' 'Ride that time!' 'No Fear'
That's the rules, kingpins rule,
See the lil' boys making big boy moves
Laughing at tramps picking cigarette butts of the
ground
B.M.'s give their kids licks for acting like clowns

I travel on bus wherever I gotta be to make P,
Man like me, graft constantly
Hand to mouth tired of it, honestly,
Wish for Rap I could charge a monster fee
Love life but could do with a change,

New complaint's how money turned all of us barmy
Charging down the Ring Road in an Artic Ferrari, right
hand on the wheel left hand on a sarnie
I'm not even driving, but there's suttin' about doing
90' that I gotta get hands on and pedal through the
night
Maybe 'cos it's the decade I found my first love
When I die, they'll say I did it my way
I'm a product of Chapeltown Academy
Victim of white mentality, but won't be a casualty.

KING OF THE UNIVERSE

By Princess Emmanuelle (EmpresS *1)

You do think you're the King.
You do think that you rule.
Think you own everything.
Think all you see is yours,
All I see is yours.
Everything around you is owned by you.
I'm entitled to what you give me,
What you show me,
and what you dress me.
You're entitled to me.
Entitled to what you want,
What you see, and what you breathe.
My mind, my body and my soul is all for you,
Merely your toys,
Your voice,
Your choice
To take.
To use and abuse,
Treat and mis-treat how and when you like.
You do think you're the King.
You do think that you rule,
Think you can have everything
To keep as if it's yours,
To keep as if I'm yours.
But I'm not,
Not yours not for you to own.
And you're not,
Not the King,
Not the ruler of this Universe as you like to think.

All you see is not for you to keep, < Please let this line
start on the new page>
All that's around you,
Don't deserve it to surround you
Don't deserve it to have found it
Don't deserve it!
You're not King,
-What, without a Queen?
Without a conscious mind,
Just a cold heart all mean.
What do you have?
What can you offer?
Who can you heal?
And do you really bother?
Those are the things you should ask yourself,
These are the things you need,
Do you know what you must possess in yourself?
Before you go ahead and breed?
You do know that you're not King
And you know that you do not rule
What are you worth, Maybe one chilling?...
Really you're just a fool!

HEROIN-KILLS!

By redeyefeenix

A new plague manufactured by human greed,
I see it every day, watching my people fiend,
Zombified will-power, non-existent,
It seems our generation failed to resist it,
Every other day we get cursed with death,
Deteriorating faces with no control left,
An unseen evil, creeping on us all.
Taking life after life, I've seen to many fall!
It starts with temptation, a choice we all make,
But then I've never seen an addict realise a mistake,

Brainwashed by smack, they will do anything they can,
I've known some scum steal from their own mam,
Consequences don't exist when you're hooked,
There's no remorse, because your mind is corrupt,
Imagine what it's like to have no self-respect,
Or pride, dignity and a damaged intellect,
Well that's exactly what I see, every time I turn around,
They could refer to Hull as heroin town,
It's a killer infestation that has to be stopped,
And if I had my way, I would end the whole lot!

Some say it's the parents' responsibility,
But it's the individual who chooses how to be,
And guess what's just around the corner from me,
They started giving out methadone for free,
I was like, "HELL NO!" we never got no free weed,

Plus they sell the methadone, and then proceed,
To get their next score, as they start to sweat,
Panicking and shaking, but do not forget,
To provide a substitute can only bring more shame,
I say, lock them in a room and let them suffer in pain,
Then maybe a percentage would stop and think twice,
Throw the way the needle, start appreciating life,

All it takes is someone to miss their vain,
Then they slowly, but surely, will die in pain,
But me, I can hope and pray,
My family and friends will see a better day,
At the minute though, I'm just watching the neighbourhood decay,
Syringes strew the streets where we used to play,
It's unbelievable how things have progressed,
From happiness, to stress, to this awful mess!

LOVE IS BLIND

By Denetta D3 Copeland

Bang!
An explosion that just can't be contained - The dice is
rolled
Apparently I'm playing the game
Concept is sit down and open your veins
Let people prod, just to be positive you're feeling the
pain
So they open up my head and walk round my brain
Even though it was found clean, now it's covered in
stains
Drop me naked - Trembling in the pouring rain
Slap my face and tell me that, I've gotta play again.
I've been wondering what all this was supposed to
gain
This insane operation is inhumane
Only to be informed
"This is just a common complaint"
They smiled like they were sitting being entertained
Saying, "Now the procedure is pre-ordained"
Like little links connected on a messed up chain
Don't beat around the bush - The message is plain
You're no longer master of your own domain.

Like a hairline fracture growing over time
Separating all the segments of my mind
Reduce me to an inch - And give me mountains to
climb
I try to break free but it seems that I'm confined

In a world of space and rhyme
I find my body filled with strength and weakness combined
Falling uncontrollably as my faith declines
But my feet keep moving 'cos my love is blind.
So I muster all the faith and logic I can find
I'm dealing with the worlds most unrefined
I'm sure you know the kind - Always on your spine
Creeping up on unsuspecting souls - From behind
Moving in slow motion now the papers are signed
And I can't fast forward or press rewind
Feeling my way in the dark - Light no longer shines
But you can't walk away with something I consider mine.

So I got myself an army 'cos I'm ready to fight
Calling anybody interested to help in my plight
Concentrating information to strengthen my bite
I fill my life with knowledge to set yours alight
Ignite everyone involved until they're burning bright
I for one am sick of trying to be polite
Deep breath...
Take aim and shoot on sight
I know there must be only one left standing tonight
Then the four corners of my universe can reunite
Light will return, welcomed by my heart's delight
Ill wrap it up in cotton wool and hold on tight
Absorbing all the wrongs and try to make them right
I know...
I'm not the one who should be feeling contrite
There's my dirty slate - You can give it a wipe
This colourful world is grey - Not black and white
And I don't deserve this trait - Put that in your pipe

THE ENEMY WITHIN

By Shaun Clarke aka Shaun MC

They say, "Keep your enemies close,"
But what happens when they get too close,
And I smell a rotten apple,
What if the enemy's within?
Under your skin, provoking, manipulating,
Confiscating, remonstrating,
Speaking on your behalf while you sleep,
Stirring with complication, in need of confrontation
Addicted to trouble and strife,
Like an ill satisfied ghost refusing to respect life,
They hijack our pilots and lead us astray,
Letting nothing get in their way,
And they'll be no signs of conflict resolution.

The show must go on, but for how much longer?
Tripped up when you're not looking, dissed when you are,
Who needs enemies or even frenemies,
When like a virus they're already embedded within?
Driven to destroying their own with tricks and delusions,
Brain and soul washing tactics.
Rewarded with dangling social snacks,
They think it's worth the sacrifice,
Humanity and chivalry,
Taking advantage of your humility.
They silence you when you have something important to say,

Something logic says is crucial,
Yet when they have trivial matters, you must drop
everything and take heed,
When deep inside you'll never agree.

Narcissistic, they need to be put in their place,
To be expelled, their arrogance buried in the wild
wind.
With flawed purpose, the enemy will deny your
perspective,
Shake, rattle and roll your world while torturing your
nerves,
You and me, we're weak, susceptible to defeat,
As they mistreat, their mission almost complete
Magically, they appear to have an edge,
Like they were sponsored and you weren't.
They played nicely, loyal and complicit,
Loved programming like wasting time and money, as
if it was all joke.
And they love the game,
The occasional thirty seconds of fame,
While resistant I remain where you can never claim it
was me...
That enemy within.

They're within, dwelling while selling out,
Like a gin, making the most of living in sin,
And we struggle against it like we can't win
He, she, they, it, her or him
May take advantage, living like a Queen or king,
With nothing in a heart made of tin,
Could be your brother, sister, Lover, or next of kin,
Sleeping in your bed and stealing your heat,

Depressing until you give in.

Deep within, doing their crazy thing,
May have the cash to splash in your face,
Put you on a lead that sets your pace,
Freedom swapped for voluntary servitude,
Protest need not apply,
Your values and nature unable to intrude,
Your own name in blood you must sign,
Time is money and your subsistence is time
Overshadowed by shallow belief,
A conditioned response,
Overcome by the abstract thief.

The enemy is within, once you let it in.
Crafty, they switch according to mainstream output.
We slip up as our children witness negativity,
While we're distracted by domestics or war, or
rumours of war.
Disrupted by death threats,
New age mental slaves are not brave,
Better crave a cave than a sick rave,
Or new age cage,
Turning a page as I rage,
Just maybe it's not all gravy.

You thought you'd bought your own blood,
But like in Hollywood, the hero came to risk all,
As it was better to die with honesty and love, than
money and pride.
The power that paper wealth brings was never going
to buy every soul.
Broken Families are could-be avoidable tragedies,

Thwarted destinies in need of constructive strategies,
Destructive sanity caught up in calamitous vanities,
Just be ready…
Your very own child might rebel.

We only remember the antagonists so we can be astonished,
frown and wonder.
Naturally, we try to remember the good guys, the heroes.
Don't be both mine and your own worst enemy, potentially
It's bad enough that I could already be my own.

AGE OF APATHY

By Louis Mcintosh

Now we're living in the Age of Apathy
A thousand Facebook friends we never see
Shit has hit the fan affecting me
As we vegetate on reality TV
Don't let it be, don't let it be, No

Listen to your conscience, listen to your soul
When you follow passion, let pension go

It's not about ME, ME
It's not about ME, ME

It's not about ME,ME
It's not your role
Listen to your conscience, listen to your soul
Now we're living in the Age of Apathy
Now we're living in the Age of Apathy

All around Catastrophe
All around Calamity
What we need is Unity
Cos we're living in the Age of Apathy
Please don't let it be
Please don't let it be

ADDICTION

By Steve Duncan

I've mesmerised and mystified
The mystics of the ancient wise
And I've baffled the greatest doctorates and
scientific minds
of our synchronised time .
Because I exist in the spirit of the greatest conspiracy.
They call me Addiction.
I am the disease
I am The I am of all I ams.
I'm the triumphant ego building scam.
I'm the insidious illusion colluding to confuse your
plans.
I'm the Kamikaze Kidnapping of the mind
And the whole attention span.

I'm the preoccupation ransom payment plan.
I've captivated feelings, but I'm promising freedom,
Release and relief in ease and comfort, peace of
mind
But paradoxically I'm a compulsive impulse
To indulge in seductive suicide.
I'm that two faced devil - playing serpents grace.
The apparently choice-less voice of fate.
I'm the delightful sight of Eve's apple.
I'm that first high, the deceptive lie,
The justification, The excuse, The alibi.
The rationalisation and gratification of temptation,
Arousing the angst anxious appetite for destruction.

I'm that sinister sinfulness
That swerves amidst the glitz and the glamour.
I'm that cocky tipsy smarmy swagger.
I'll exalt you to the stars and watch you flutter to the gutter
Captured in that Wrath of rapture
Rolling reefers to revert you to the grim reaper.
I'm pleased when you're six feet beneath
Receiving wreaths and I've blessed you with diseases.

I am the degradation, The desolation,
The destroyer of species, Them legions of leaches
The suckers that succumb to blood sucking scum,
Those intravenous vein-less creatures.
The obsessive obese beast,
The gluttonous over-eating feast of fury.
The overdose obnoxious gross negligent prone
Home to the luck lustrous infrastructure
Of self centred pleasure.
The me, myself and I,
Self will run riot that kills, Animal instinct.
Seven deadly sinned thrilling Fatal fairground attraction.
I'm that roller coaster ride that's never satisfied.
I'm the dodgem of death, The waltzer of woes,
The carousel of cravings.
I'm the candy floss that moulds and metamorphoses
Into different flavours, tastes,
Then shapes the behaviour.
I make manifest in food and sex
And cyber-net connects, Repetitive texts,
Gambling, shopping and credit card debts,
I'm that twist in the very fabric of nature

Extracting the worst aspects of your character.

I'm that spiritual death,
The targeted defective hit,
The emotional eclipse.
The prickle in the prick of a pin
Shooting at the speed of light
Laughing at the harm reduction rate
Of hero to heroin and prostitute to pimp.
I'm the grouch, The chained and untamed.
And you know I'm the nose
That nobody knows
Better than cocaine.
Nonsensical, false pretence
Alcoholic bum and bench mentality.
Im that crack in the perception of perceptive reality.
The mirror image mirage of cosmetic insanity.
I'm the ugliest form of vanity,
The most profound profanity.
This curious calamity,
The debacle of debauchery,
Debonair delusion of a distorted personality.

I'm non partial, prejudicial to scale or class,
Surpassing the vastness of intellect, culture, creed or
race.
Debasing the face value of shame.
I savagely shift the equilibrium of relationships,
And with all things being equal,
Emotional appeal wont seal my prevention .
I'm sibling separation, Maternal manipulation,
The evil revelation in in all relations.
I'm the devil's advocation

Of the never ending end
of all things bright and beautiful .
I'm beyond the bond and above the above.
Because I am Addiction
And when I'm active
I'm stronger than love.
See, I'm taller than tall
And all I call, one and all
Will fall before Me.
Because Hell have no fury on humanity like I.
Because I am fly
The fly through thief in the night,
That soars higher than hindsight.
But I'll never get to heaven.
So I'm hovering somewhere
between defence and consequence.

I'm sitting on a fence of Moral resolution,
A slithering, conniving, sliding snake,
Spitting venom at the solution.
I'm that slippery slope
The hazardous hole,
Waiting for you to fall
So I can take control.
I mix and blend, cocktail carousing.
Patiently waiting for the party.
Send invitations under the guise of the befriended,
From time beyond, until time extended,
Until the intervention of God's revenge
I will exist as a gift in the present.
So stay awake to my presence.
Because I am the phenomenon
The Beast, Of Addiction.

HUMAN NATURE
(Love & Hate)

SOMEDAY

By Denetta D3 Copeland

'Cos you made me
But the universe said that you couldn't stay
It's amazing
That I can see with these tears in my way
I am grieving
I need to believe that there is a place
Will you be in if I just decided to pass by?
Someday...

Do you see me?
Invisible you standing by my side
Are you feeling... as depleted as I do, inside?
What you gave me is it enough to keep me awake?
Overtaking
A natural desire to follow you away
Someday...

Who will be there?
I'm patiently waiting with anticipation
For answers to my prayers
Gracing my presence, sent straight from heaven
Imagine your face when you see that it's me
knocking at your door
A warm embrace...
... to die for
Someday...

WHAT'S SO DIFFERENT?

*Princess Emmanuelle (EmpresS *1)*

Festival Fastings, Festival Feastings,
Veil on the head, and families meeting,
Eid celebrations, Christmas and Easter,
Praising a prophet, saint or spiritual leader.
Values of living so similar in essence,
Morals of kindness, forgiveness, and loving,
Peace and equality, patience is a blessing.
Know thyself and appreciate all that is living.

What's so different? What's so different?
Between him or her
What's so different? What's so different?
Between here and there
What's so different?
If you're Muslim, or if you're Christian
A label to your name, but there's not much
difference!

Mother Earth was not created 4 just u, u, u,
It was also not create for jus' a few, few, few,
Different cultures, tribes and groups
I hear u boo, boo, boo,
Different languages and looks,
Spirituality 'n Religions too.
Are you really, are you really open minded, are you?
Humble and respectful with integrity to?
Are you biased with your views, prejudice with ur
actions,

Then jus ready to chat 'n put up the Unity caption?!

What's so different? What's so different?
Between him or her
What's so different? What's so different?
Between here and there
What's so different?
If you're Ethiopian, or if you're Egyptian
A label to your name, but there's not much
difference!

I know a place that we all come from
1 Jah, Rabena, Igzeyabaar, Allah,
It's 1Love, 1Peace, 1Life
It's a blessing
Why so many fuss 'n fight ignoring spiritual lessons…
Laws of the Spirit r simply Universal,
Don't lie, don't cheat, don't hurt, no deceit,
When you meet with a blessing make sure u
appreciate it,
Cos if you don't stay pure you kno' you gonna pay
for it.

U like Yellow, I like Lavender,
He like Green, but she likes none of them,
I speak Egyptian, U speak Amharic,
She speaks Chinese, They speak sign language.

Oi Tudo bem?
Tenayistillin yo!
Igzeyabaar Yamasgaan
Kierialayson
Languages differ like your hands and feet

But we still understand Love
Now let's all say Ameen

What's so different? What's so different?
Between him or her
What's so different? What's so different?
Between here and there
What's so different? If you're Muslim, or if you're
Christian
A label to your name, but there's not much
difference!
What's so different?
Between him or her
Between here and there
What's so different?
If you're Ethiopian, or if you're Saudi
A label to your name, but there's not much
difference!

BATCHELOR BLUES

By Louis Mcintosh

I am a bachelor, I am free,
What's for dinner, what's for tea?
Whatever I please, whatever I please.
I am a bachelor, look at me,
Smartly dressed in my own stylee,
Loadsamoney earnt by me, to spend on who? That's easy... me,
Whenever I please, whenever I please.
I am a bachelor by choice you see,
Though every woman fancies me
But I can't commit there's more to see
I am a bachelor, I am free, I am selfish, Me, Me, me

It's all about me, It's all about me
I am a bachelor lonely as can be,
I've had my fun, don't pity me
Got no kids, no family tree,
but I've got a new car and flat screen TV
Is it all about me? Not sure you see
I am a bachelor, tell me sincerely, does everybody envy me?
And if they don't, what's life for me, is there really more to see?
Before I'm old and unhappy...
Save me, something save me, please.

A sperm, an egg, million to one
A test result, new life begun

Where there was one, now there are three
An unborn child, mother and me
And so I bid the old life bye, awaiting baby's primal cry
The bachelor has had his day, life part two awaits some say
With boundless love and wordless joy
No matter, whether girl or boy
The belly swells, the hormones swirl, got your mother in a whirl
I'm ready, what will be, will be.
On being Dad, it's not about me....finally.

SORRY

By Shamile Haline

In the night time, all around
See your face,

Silly words come back to me now
See my mistakes.

My fears showed the worse of me

My fears took away my destiny

The nights are long…

As I watch the midnight skies
Please forgive my foolish pride.

I'm so sorry…

URBAN
WORLD/JUNGLE/DESTINY
(Creative journeys through living)

CULTIVATE

By Nadinne Dyen (In respect to Phife Diggy)

Disolving words of wisdom,
Locked up and hidden,
Selling us off with schisms,
Dividing and diluting,
Self-knowledge and intuition,
Give me fyah to blaze,
Bring back golden hip hop days,
Through rhythm, rhyme and melodic phrase,
Eternally I praise,
Setting pages on Fyah,
Ablaze,
Intense,
Incense,
Spiritual smoke,
Clearing my head,
Guiding me through the
Numerological maze,
Nor affected or dazed,
By this constant celebrity craze,
Producers producing the same,
Unoriginal verbal gangster clichés,
Creatively I blaze,
Sun-worshipers,
Cradled by solar rays,
Maternally I gaze,
Blazing sun,
Mother of all,
Eye of Allah,

Guardian of Universal Law,
Ignorance of man,
In fight for the Wailing Walls,
Pain staking cries of children of Palestine calls,
Prey for the arms merchandisers to fall,
Crumble and bawl

Yet,
Mama always taught me not to follow a path,
Go instead where there's no trails,
Make your own trail,
Inhail,
The Ashe energy,
Ifa religion,
Yoruba cosmology,
Keeping check of cognitive psychology,
Development and over-standing of Self
Methodology,
Linking your personal stories like geometry,
To ancient Mythology

Yet,
Go down into the abyss is where the treasure hides,
Where you stumble is where the treasure lies.
Realize that real eyes, see real lies.
Don't be paralyzed by back-stabbing allies,
Needs must
You must walk alone,
Hollow torso of emptiness, that subsides with this
loneliness,
My walk alone, brought me to my queenliness,
My empress,
Not to impress

My walk alone,
Sourcing my internal home
Too ...

Innovate, Cultivate, Create, Shape, Design,
Actualize,
Prophesize, Not hypothesize, Organise,
Bring to existence, Manifest your vision,
Originate, Not imitate, Create, Bring birth your
dreams, Supreme,
Bring forth Life

Taboo,
Misrepresentations of Africa,
Voodoo,
Internal Guru,
You Choose,
As much as there is nothing,
There is everything
Seeking Wisdom of Solomon the King,
Remembering everything is everything,
Is how it's been designed.
Keep eyes open wide,
Cause life is one big road with a lots of signs
Listening for the Parables,
Process parallels
Opening the Channels
Reflecting the wings of your angel,
Will enable,
Stable
Eyezzzzzzz, to see,
To impede the image Lucifer,
Checking ego's as big a Jupiter,

Bit early to be,
Entombing ya,
Crucify ya,
Memories,
Dreams,
Reflections,
Prays,
Calling upon the ancestors
Again eternally I praise,

Law of gravity, we are ever falling,
Searching for our calling
Humans yearning to fly, never grateful or satisfied,
NASA spending billions, to buy up the sky
What goes up, must come down,
This Mountainous road makes us all individual and
profound,
Law of significance,
As a poet seeing the world with a difference
Although we are all poets,
That can share and verbalise,
Our perspective differently.

Through our ever poetic eyes,
Ocean pearls line the sky,
Sea of stars,
Cosmic planes in which we can dance,
Enhance,
Tackle the insane,
Cleanse in the holy water,
Sub-Saharan Rain,
Expanding the 10 percent usage of our of our brains
Regain,

To ...

Innovate, Cultivate, Create, Shape, Design,
Actualize,
Prophesize, Not hypothesize,
Organise,
Bring to existence, Manifest your vision,
Originate, Not imitate, Create, Bring birth your
dreams, Supreme,
Bring forth Life,
YOU ARE LIFE

YOU
ARE
LIFE

B BOY & GIRL STANCE
(Where it's at)

By Shaun Clarke aka Shaun MC

Born of Kool Herc breaks and them who shared his
mentality,
Touched by heart and vision, we commenced on a
journey
From past to present, unknowing this force was
unstoppable
You might have forgiven others for thinking he was
mad
But madness turned out to be a genius, or so it often
goes
An accident or reawakening?
A dreamy pass time united us through cohesion and
circumstance.
Top rock, six step, power move and freeze, a lingo
now popular as Bingo,
Proving the world is not just in the hands of the few
Poppin', Lockin', B-Boppin' - Electric Boogaloo,
Fab Five Freddy, New York City Breakers and the rock
steady crew,
to name a few
Legends of electros and funky break beats such as
Man Parish, Grandmaster Flash and The Furious Five
infected the UK
Spreading into my city it became my world.
Suddenly my people were everywhere.

I had little loose change but belonged to a timeless

tribe called quest
Internationally it grew and persisted
Leaving early critics with nothing left to say
While we show respect always due to the originals,
our distant relatives
Under pressure to break out of the box, like a cell
within the body, which when attacked, mutates for
the sake of survival.
Fed by the African American and Puerto Rican spirits,
Hip Hop and Funk-it-up grew like a tree, a way to be
free,
For them excluded from capitalistic cultural
opportunity.
A styled out movement replaced street gang
warfare,
From an urge to bust out of suppression.

A beat boxer, some trainers, a tracksuit or something
like a cagoule,
A hat for protection, and a synchronized, dancing
heart beat submerged in the culture,
A fine Kangol looked the part and kept your head
warm
A journey to find yourself, alternative to crime,
violence, boredom and drugs, if only for a time.
A bridge to a better life that included ultimate fitness
and life-long lessons like self-discipline.
Self-inflicted pain, always in order to gain,
Like muscles and the feel good factor, friends, and
only the sort of foes that would excite and motivate
to get better.

They lay the foundations for the future

Some gain strength to earn due respect
This kind of street-cred makes one worthy of praise,
In a space where cash prizes can mean nothing
This is about identity, being recognised as a true
practitioner with roots, recognition and authenticity
People are left in awe as they wonder about the
elusive,
That internalised swagger - that crazy move.

Yet we're devout, because this is part of who we are.
It saved lives, brought some from the brink, and must
be awarded that accolade.
Evolved to mainstream entertainment, once, then
again, its legacy lives on
Sold out, as every fad tends to, diluted and polluted
for finance,
But its core is perpetual, a sure place from where it
came,
A flame that will never fade, and the world will look
back.
"Keep it real," some will say, "Like we kept it real,"
that is; staying true to yourself and the art form,
And If you only have one leg or arm, work with that,
Destiny will take care of the rest
And one day, you may be lucky enough to make it to
your unique style.
Confidence bred from observers who show some
love,
You could be doing a lot worse than tricks with your
own anatomy,
Making others gasp, so impressed like a fan they'll
support you and your scene.

Warriors in dance battles, they move forward, not back, offensive from the trenches, but they wait and wonder, contemplate and ponder about going yonder, beyond the lines, but only when the time to strike is right.

While the breaks and cuts, old skool blend into new
Yet in freestyle contest nothing can be perfect unless a show is staged,

There's only perfect timing when your moment comes,

When it all comes together...

"WOW! Did you see dat mad move! That was sick!"
That's the spirit of this boy or that girl,
And in the end there remains, this or that respect and love.

POETIC PRESCRIPTIONS

By Empress Imani

Without an outlet for this type of expression
It could equal constant soul regression
And many hiding their true profession
As it aids one's own conquest of self-progression.
My soul knows I need this
Ask the bandages, they will tell you I bleed for this.

Sometimes I get caught up in a vast abyss
In my subconscious state where my essence exists
Intertwined with my conscious mind and hovering in
different paradigms
Seeking to defy the rules and extend time
To scratch the surface and form new lines, for I hold
true words close to my chest
Wearing my bulletproof vest

Like a loaded gun I relentlessly empty out the very
best of me.
Make a right turn till there's nothing .... left of me.
It's like fully comprehending, this newly discovered
form of spiritual cleansing,
Like pins and needles in my side, pricking me ten
thousand times,
My therapy lies between the lines of these rhymes,
reminding me nothing died in me but I'm still alive.

As these droplets of my thought patterns
Just happen to awake my conceptual zones.

The vibrational tones form new clones,
I'm in escape mode.
Dreaming of fleeing to a place
Where I can rest my feet on a map at the door of my
third eye that says....
Welcome home!
Reminding me that I'm never alone.
Giving me free expression within this humble space.
A sacred infinite guarded place
Where the scrolls of my existence cannot be
replaced,
Cannot be altered and cannot be erased.

I want to reach into your solar plexus and take grip,
Attempt to encrypt, my words in your flesh like a
microchip.
Not for means of control, but to give you freedom to
think.
Vivid visual perception every time that you blink.
Open the vortex of your mind, so your concepts don't
shrink.
As I battle with the resilience of change coming
soon.
I marvel at the brilliance of my butterfly wings,
As before I was nestled in my cocoon,
But now I beam so bright,
I can afford to dim my light so at night I can be your
Moon!
Shine!
And to bear the remnants of your soul is never a
crime.

Many enact a pact for my soul to retract

And attempt to enrol me in creative rehab,
But I will always relapse,
Because I will express my words until my lungs collapse.
Not for finger snaps or hand claps,
But to free my mind from these mental traps.
Decode the script so it's no longer an act.
I've suffered hypocritical contradictions, social restrictions and spiritual inflictions,
But in the sickness of society's aimless addictions.
All I need is a few written up poetic prescriptions.

HIP HOP VERSE

By Redeyefeenix

You're my Hip-Hop, I feel you deep within my soul,
My breeze when it is hot, my warmth when it is cold,
You're my life story, happiness and pain creates you,
My life saver, one thing I can relate too,
My chosen path, I want you more than anything,
You're my destiny, my queen
So proud to be your king

You're my alter ego, and what a journey it's been,
My inspiration, take me places never seen,
You're my first love, my passion, my personality,
I wear my mic on my sleeve, if you want to battle me,
You're my legacy, the only way, Daz might hear me,
And if not, I play his song when I need him near me,
You're my dream, my fire, my burning desire,
That's why I'll be rocking the mic till I retire,

You're my Hip-Hop, you made me the r-e-d,
Representing Hull City most beautifully,
You're my guidance keep me from temptation and
crime,
My side line, keeping me keen until I've got mine,
You're my conscience, help me put to paper my
thoughts,
My education, but with music it's self-taught,
You're my inner beast, so I keep you locked up,
Hoping you don't escape, undetected from all of us,
You're my company, you have never left my side,

And if you did, I would be devastated, that's no lie,
You're my oil to my engine, pedal to my motor,
Key to my ignition, my food, and my water,
You're my hope, my lifestyle, my direction,
My dope, my support, and redemption,
You're my future, my present, and my past,
My full time care worker, always got my back,
You're my wildcard, my all, in my full pot!
My everything, I love you... You're my Hip-Hop!

RESISTANCE
Peacemakers V the warmongers

ECLIPSE

By Testament

Now is the hour when the darkness reigns
'Cause we can't see how things can start to change
In the moon's masquerade, fools charm their way
Entombed between the rock and the hardest place
The harshest fate, my mood's past the heavy weight
But we too are lost in the vast array
Even the sun meditates on a martyr's wage
In the eclipse I remember words my father said:
He said "Sleep was a gift from God" and sometimes
You look around at the world and you can see why
I awake and this too will pass away
Withering like flames around the lunar face

And yes, it's looking grim, but I'm another reaper
Sow the storm, reap the wind, words from the
preacher
Tonight's feature, hurled across the firmament
Between souls in this lost universe where light gets
weaker
The tower teeters, and a second dawn approaches
They reckon all it takes is time to heal emotions, but
that's bogus
I take a hold of the hopeless; the night rolls on the city
strobes with commotion
The earth's groaning, you catch the shift in your
shoulders
Blink in the eclipse? Nah, my eyes wide open
Without light I'm never satisfied with the moment

But my mind is my greatest opponent

It's like I'm holding onto dreams in the middle of
nightmares
Stood in the darkness but the answer's in the bright
glare
Right there, so I set my hope on what's better than
gold
Heaven knows, you know the devil don't fight fair
Kinda scared, you cannot meddle with fate
Too busy fighting with myself and all these venomous
snakes
She tells me of pain, remember the birth pains
Tremble and shake but still many never relate
But God's light makes you levitate, forget this anguish
Yes indeed there is a method to the madness
The night sky above me is candlelit, cavernous
Scattering these tears until we vanish

UNITED PLIGHT

By Justin Swaby

Feeling like stuck in belly of the beast
Thorn in the side can rupture with ease
Snipping head shots like a photo-cop
Lost the plot, time to stop, change face photo-shop

War in the world, too deep
Ammunitions need deplete ceased many wanting to eat
Greedy most central banking familiars
Mafia's regaining control, keep hold of your soul
Do not click-sign on the dotted line
Contract arranged in haste, leads to waste

Focus on the positive and good in life
Will help to cool your mind
When faced with strife

More fire more fire until peace reigns
Another coming like the third Reich
Time for the globe to unite
We share the same plight
Like Michael Jackson sung, "It doesn't matter if your black or white"
Coypu in delight with every sight
Then we just might
Make it together out of this flight of the phoenix.

PROMISED LAND

By Michael Jenkins - Lowdose

I wanna go right back
To the land of the blacks
But our mind states weak
That's why we fight on the streets
Daily, gotta deal with the devilish beast
Always wanting a piece
Dem a blood-clart leech

From Uganda to Zimbabwe
Me a take it back, or it's bum bye yae
It's a myth cos we're not inferior
From Egypt to Mali, Nigeria
Were far from poor, so don't believe the media
That's why they fighting in Libya
Desperately needing resources
So all I see is Trojan horses
One meal a day
Dem a yam 3 courses
Living nice, while my people live awkward
Teefing the minerals to build up I-phones and
Porsches
Make sure problems don't get sorted

Make the truth over distorted.
War criminals come home and get applauded
But it's written in stone, that's where it's recorded
I can't sell out
I've already been exported

Extorted
I might get deported back
To the promised-land

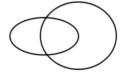

BOMBS AWAY

By Louis Mcintosh

Finger on the trigger not a finger on the pulse
Meddle with the Truth so what you pedal's False
Conscience in reverse while your brain is stuck in gear
Give the people what you want - unhealthy Dose of
Fear

So chocks away, Bombs away, how many kids will you
kill today?
Chocks away, Bombs away, Who will pay, Who will
pay?
In those Lands so far away

Safety first, safety first, make sure they will come off
worst,
While we're safely tucked in bed, clean and dry and
warm, well fed
Don't look too hard you'll see the cracks in what they
say are cold, hard facts.

So chocks away, Bombs away, get down on your
knees and pray
Life's not black and white, it's Grey
Will the Innocent last the day?

Isis this and Isis that, they're here, they're there, look
under mat
We shoot, they move, we move, they shoot
Who can win, we all will lose

Take a step back, ruminate
Fight fire with fire is obstinate

So chocks away, Bombs away
Live to breathe another day
If only we put Bombs away
If only we put Bombs away
Bombs away

MAD WORLD

By redeyefeenix

The world's a crazy place to live in
Destruction everywhere,
War after war people dead
We do not care,
We just accept it because that's how we are
programmed,
It's ok to kill a man as long as it's for land,

Year after year, the world's people live in fear,
Death on their mind, life filled with pain and tears,
But where's the justice, is there any in the world?
I see paedophiles getting three years for hurting little
girls,
For this I say bring back hanging! Or even better yet,
Let them loose with the parents, let them beat them
to death,

If the government do not care, what's the people to
do?
Trust me there's nobody to help you in this world, just
you,
Stand on your own feet, use your will to survive,
Control your own destiny, you must live your own life,

This country is a joke
It's hard to use your vote
Great Britain,
What's great about a country that is broke....

SCIENCE
(Arriving at the present – future)

REMOTE CONTROLLED

By Shamile Haline

I'm a flash, I'm an advert
Just another...
Mechanical man
I'm sick, I'm choking
These values, I just don't understand
Remote Controlled,
Remote Controlled

You're direction is my vision
I am your thoughts

Who am I? What am I?
Embryos are confused, still they multiply
Please don't try to change, we've come too far
Please don't try to rearrange, we've gone too far

Remote Controlled,
Remote Controlled

DAWN OF SINGULARITY

By Shaun Clarke aka Shaun MC

Get me a robot and I'll give it a job,
And I don't intend to become a slob
Don't need it for love, or even friendship
But it can work hard when I need a kip
Do a few sums, wash up, or warm my food,
Don't give me a robot that's going to be rude.

Let it be, that we all can work a lot less,
While machines simply do what they do best,
Technological world, do me a favour,
Keep in movies that ill behaviour,
Whether murderous lasers, or light-sabers,
We can't let these robots be our saviours.

Bots should give us more space and time
Every one of us may feel just fine
Isn't it time to look out for each other?
All of us, like true sisters and brothers
Hand us more convenience to find true lovers
Give us a break while we think about others.
Let's make use, and not a abuse them,
Not be silly, and try confuse them
I'm not against them, we don't want to lose them
Thing about bots, you don't have to amuse them.

Singularity, won't you come in peace
Working together would be a relief
For me and you, and the rest of our kind

Let's do this, since we've been losing our mind.
Come the dawn of singularity, let's get it right
May we realise we don't have to fight,
And we might just address everyone's plight,
Especially since evolution's in sight.

We can't let the bad guys keep control,
With a hellraising fear that has taken hold
Their ideas to follow are much too old
We can't let the future be bought and sold.
Let us align like planets and stars,
With our super-trains and intelligent cars,
Holidays like fantastic trips to mars,
(Whatever we do...)
Let's keep our robots shut in their jars.

GLOSSARY
(In alphabetical order)

- *Allah (Muslim and Christian God)*
- *Ameen (Expressing agreement with God's truth)*
- *Ashe (Divine <u>energy</u>, the <u>Creator</u> and sun of the Yorbuba people of Nigeria)*
- *Bein' (Human being)*
- *Bots (Robots)*
- *Brares (Brothers)*
- *Bum bye yae (To kill)*
- *Chems (Synthetic drugs)*
- *Coypu (Climax)*
- *Dat (That)*
- *Ifa (The ceremonial. Nigerian life. Human destiny "rooted in the breath of God Almighty)*
- *Igzeyabaar (Thanks be to God – Amharic, Ethiopian)*
- *Jah (God of Rastafarians)*
- *Joneses (The Joneses)*
- *Khnum (Egyptian deity, originally the god of the source of the Nile River)*
- *Kierialayson (Kiryalayson - Lord have mercy - Coptic)*
- *Loadsamoney (Lots of money)*
- *'llow (Allow)*
- *MAAT (Ancient Egyptian concept of truth, order, harmony, morality, and justice, personified as a goddess of the stars, seasons, and the actions of both mortals and deities, who ordered the universe from chaos)*
- *Nil grats (Money)*
- *Lungi (Sarong)*
- *Oi Tudo bem (Hello, how are you -*

Portugese)
- *Rabena (Eyptian Coptic Orthodox)*
- *Reppin' (Representing)*
- *Sket (Super Ho - Caribbean)*
- *Sir Coxone (Sound system artist)*
- *Stylee (Style)*
- *Teefing (Stealing)*
- *Tenayistillin (How are you Amharic/Ethiopian)*

From top right: Empress Imani, David Okwesia, Michael Jenkins, Denetta D3 Copeland, J Bravo, Nadinne Dyen, Karabo Moruakgomo, Silver Finger Singh, Saiqa Rehman, Louis Mcintosh, Princess Emmanuelle, InI Oneness, Steve Duncan, Shamile Haline, Testament, Shaun Clarke, Saju Ahmed, Axsom Nelson, Redeyefeenix, Justice Swaby, Edsom Burton

Contributing Writers

1. **Testament (aka Homecut)** is an MC who has collaborated with the likes of Corinne Bailey Rae and Soweto Kinch, and a well-established Spoken Word artist based in West Yorkshire. He uses Hip Hop to make a positive impact on wider culture, in live shows and workshops. He is also a theatre maker, and holds a Guinness World record for human beatboxing. (**www.homecut.co.uk**)

2. **Edson Burton** is a renowned writer and performance poet, historian and programmer, based in Bristol. To his credit he has also been acting professionally. He's thoroughly edu-taining and has been previously described as "Provocative and readable."

3. **Denetta D3 Copeland** is a spoken word (Spotlight winning) artist and writer hailing from Leeds. Aka D3, she's recognised by her lyrical styles and rhyme in her story telling. Widely recognised as a unique talent (including by the BBC), she writes and performs her own style of Ra- poetry, and works in other genres such as; House, Jungle and Drum'n'Bass. For years she has volunteered with Leeds Young Authors, determined to help young people break through all oppressive barriers. (Google Denetta D3 Copeland – Poet - Leeds)

4. **Michael Jenkins (aka Lowdose)** is a Bristol based rapper, performer and media producer,

working with 8th sense media. His (film making) company has made the first acclaimed Bristol based urban drama called 'Grade', as well as other thought provoking productions such as 'Stop Search'. Otherwise, he continues to appear both on recordings and as a live MC/Performer. (www.lowdose.co.uk)

5. **Nadinne Dyen** is Poetess "burning with inflammable purpose… A gripping performer." Based in Bristol, she's full of "awe inspiring" passion, and been making waves. She recently supported the mighty Saul Williams and then Linton Kwesi Johnson. Impactful, she, "weaves her personal experiences into a larger social context with a variety of mystical meanings, metaphors and images…" *Evening Echo*.

6. **Shaun Clarke (aka Shaun MC aka Venomoustings)** currently based in Bristol, is a journalist, novelist, and a writer of poetry, rap and songs, still involved in music wherever possible. Starting out as a humble songwriter/musician and performer, he has since collaborated with various artists including MC Speedo, Empress Imani, EmpresS*1, Kocky K, and LSK, among others. (See Venomoustings on Soundcloud, and Shaun Clarke The Writer on Facebook)

7. **Redeyefeenix** is seasoned, an internationally signed Hip-Hop artist from Kingston Upon Hull, dedicated to word-life in the form of (motivational) rap music and production. He recently won a Wisdom Award from the Universal Zulu Nation for his community

workshops over the years. His latest album 'Still Representing Hull' is out on (www.vodrecordings.net).

8. **Justin "J Bravo" Archibald** is a hip hop MC, (C.A.G member) and producer from Leeds, with a wealth of recordings and live appearances under his belt. He has contributed in various social development schemes and festivals in an effort to advocate the value of self- expression and community arts. He is currently a member of Hip Hop collective; Tha Office.

9. **Axsom Nelson (aka Matry Mcfly)** is a prolific London based rapper, live performer and recording artist, also a member of Firm Fusion. He works solo and collaborates, (has worked with Dazbeatz, Cue, Caesar, Nolay, Paigey Cakey, Stealth, Rockstar, and many others). He work often describes the challenges of surviving and reaching beyond average ambitions. (Find Matry's Official Soundcloud, or Google Matry Mcfly or Axsom Nelson)

10. **Empress Imani** is an award winning poetess, singer and song writer, a live performer and a studio recording artist, residing in Leeds. She's long had a passion for creative writing, and her purposeful, expressive soul is clearly conveyed in her spoken pieces. She has performed widely, at Leeds Carnival, CITYLINKUP, for Women in Music, and supported Luciano-Messenger at Reggae Culture-Fest. She's worked with Royal Sounds and Brown Roots Band. Sharing her work at various events and UK wide community

projects, her heart felt, deep poetic renditions have reached many.

11. **Steve Duncan (aka Steve the Poet)** is a Bristol-based award winning Spoken Word artist, Speaker, Workshop facilitator, Criminal Justice consultant and founder of Big Man Mentoring, and a playwright. He has worked at Festivals, Carnivals, Prisons, Schools and other educational facilities, and has been commissioned by the BBC and Probation Services. Co-founder of Insider Insight, he challenges perceptions around inequality, social injustice and the state of humanity. He describes his work as language of the heart.

12. **Idren Natural (aka Inl Oneness)** is a Roots Reggae MC and movement, writing and recording songs, as well as producing. Starting with Imperial Youth, he has since worked with the likes of Ashanti, Ras Muffet, Mystical Powa, and Dred and Fred, and toured internationally. Inspired by the spirit of Rastafari and Nyahbinghi, "Zulu Warrior Dub Sound and King David-music," his first recording was Highest Region, with Reuben Unitone and Jacob Naphty, released through Jah Shaka. (Google Idren Natural or Inl Oneness)

13. **EmpresS *1 (aka Princess Emmanuelle)** is "Egypt's 1st Female Egyptian Rapper" and has toured internationally, performing her Rap-Poetry. A 'Spoken Word' Poetess, she has been writing since the age of 7. Her first album; "Born into a Drowning World is ground-breaking. She has opened up for, or featured

with Jocelyn Brown, O Rappa, Public Enemy, Dawn Penn, Keith Murray, Al Griffiths, and Gyptian, among others. She also runs workshops in Creative Dance, Drama, and Word Sound n' Power. While addressing various issues, she is "holding the flag for women - under-represented… in Hip-Hop..." (Afrolution.com) Find her at; (Google EmpresS1Egypt or see princessemmanuelle.bandcamp.com/)

14. **Louis Mcintosh** is a Poet, Song Writer and Singer, as well as a recording artist. He is currently the frontman for Dubtonez band. As a creative writer and journalist he writes regularly for the Huffington Post. Further he's the author of Black Dawg. (Find Louis on Facebook, Dubtonez on Soundcloud.)

15. **Saju Ahmed** was a Slam competition winning Spoken Word artist/poet with the Leeds Young Authors. He has performed internationally and sees himself as an activist whose work attacks social problems and suggests a new way of breaking stereotypes. He has featured in documentaries; We are poets, Dyslexia and Loving Words. He has also appeared on BBC 1xtra Live Lounge with Trevor Nelson. (Search Saju Ahmed/Leeds Young Authors)

16. **Saiqa Rehman (aka Lightning Sykes)** is a bilingual rapper/poet (living in Leeds), who writes and produces her own material. She has performed in her native English and Urdu on an international stage, and to audiences at Festivals and Melas around the UK. She's also a DJ, open mic-compere/promoter, and

radio/TV hostess (Fever FM and Fever TV), in the North of England. She's a co-founder of Lyrically Justified open mic events, coordinates for the Hyde Park Unity Day and has her own recording studio. (Look for Lightening Sykes/Lyrically Justified)

17. **David Okwesia (aka Full Flava aka Redlocz)** is a rap and reggae influenced vocalist/lyricist for Dubungle (his current project), representing Hull (UK). He's also a Hip Hop entrepreneur, promoter and innovator, and currently presents the Full Flava Connection Show via West Hull FM. (www.full-flava.co.uk or find Dubungle on Soundcloud)

18. **Raj SilverFinger Singh**, a music graduate at Leeds Metropolitan University, is a Rapper/MC based in Leeds and well known for performing and music production. . His music is influenced by a fusion of Eastern rhythms and textures mixed with Western beats and flavours. He was featured on the BBC Asian Network "Raw & Ready" Radio Show with DJ Yasser. Supported the likes of Ian Brown (The Stone Roses), Punjabi MC & The Winachi Tribe. (Google SilverFinger Singh, also on Facebook)

19. **Justin Swaby (aka Wordgineer/ SoulJAH/MOTA)** won a book prize at primary school. He took poetry seriously in his late teens, when he was encouraged to perform. He first used the name SoulJAH, then became Wordgineer, then later Mission of Truth Allegiance - MOTA. (Wordgineer on Soundcloud)

20. **Karabo Moruakgomo (aka Kayb)** was born and raised in South Africa, settling in England in 2012, now based in Bristol. He has been a member of youth projects (including Envision), which have boosted his confidence. He worked with NCS Young Bristol, and has been part of Charities such as Freedom Project. He's passionate about making music. ('Karabo KB' on Facebook, Kayb on soundcloud)

21. **Shamile Haline** is a London based Songwriter/Poet. He studied music and reflects heartache for earnest love and mutual dependency. He also works in the field of challenging injustices around the world, encouraging others to stand up and be counted and helps artists struggling against the tide of exploitation. He's the creative director of Mango World.